Drink Responsibly!

A How-to Guide for Drinkers who want to cut back.

By International Bestselling Kindle Author on Suicide & Neuropsychologist:

Dr. Jacob K. Ray, Psy.D.

"Giving up is something you do for somebody else, letting go is something you do for yourself." --Anonymous quote found online.

Prologue-

You are made from stars. At your peak potential, you could be unstoppable, successful, and happy. At your worst or while addicted, you could destroy anyone or anything or you could be toxic to yourself, the world, and the people in your life. Being human means being fallible. Being an alcoholic can be benign to you but scream malignant to those around you. You can choose to ignore the cancer of addiction as it rots your soul and potential or you can grab the battle worn reigns. I don't care what you do for a living. I don't know who you are. I am in an objective spot. Let me make you reconsider drinking like an insatiable alcoholic and consider being an alcohol enthusiast. The difference is you will be regifted the power of choice.

When you control alcohol and not the other way around you have this experience called fun. Fun is fun. Being a hardcore drunk is no fun. The fallout from your tragic, idiotic, psychotic behavior will snowball on you. You can't escape it. Melt the snowball by apologizing to everybody who still speaks to you. Tell them you are trying this new method and if you fail, you are going to rehab to quit alcohol.

If you fail at my method, go to rehab. If you have already been to rehab or Alcoholics Anonymous, stay clean. My method is for the well-adjusted, hard working, regular paycheck cashing, no legal history with alcohol "heavy drinker" who has grown weary of having bad nights. If you are drinking all day everyday or have the daily shakes for a drink, my method won't work for you. If any doctor, therapist, social worker, boss or legal professional (police, judge, probation officer, lawyer) has required you to stop drinking but you won't, my method is not for you. Quit.

Use the CAGE screen to determine if you are an alcoholic: Have you ever tried to Cutback? Have others Annoyed you by criticizing your drinking? Have you ever felt Guilty about your drinking? Do you sometimes start the day off with an Eye-opener drink to cure a hang over or get going? Thank you, Dr. John Ewing, for developing the CAGE questionaire. In 1984, he wrote 'Detecting Alcoholism: The CAGE Questionaire' in the *Journal of the American Medical Association 252: pages 1905-1907*. If you answered "Yes" to any of the questions, stop living in that CAGE, break free by quitting. If you are a liquor drinker or have severe, detox-worthy alcoholism, my method won't work due to poor impulsivity regulation on your part. If you have ever gotten violent with anybody while drunk, my method won't work due to poor impulse regulation on your part. If you are on any other drugs like cocaine, pills, heroin, speed, and/or any other substance that you use habitually or occasionally, my method won't work. If you have harmed yourself while drinking or are suicidal and using anything, it won't work. If you cannot or do not adhere to my method, it won't work.

Being an alcohol enthusiast is only for the well-adjusted. You need to have a job, a regular income, a place to live that you pay for, no legal problems around alcohol, no major detrimental addiction problems in life and the foresight to know that by investing in this life long change that you will never drink too much again, for your own preservation. If you were born with or acquired severe mental health issues, my method is likely to be more trouble than its worth. If you are on any medication (including all psychiatric drugs) and your doctor told you not to drink on them but you do it anyway, my method is not for you. You should quit.

Lastly, I am in no way liable, responsible, accountable, or in control of anything you do while drinking. Readers must be of legal drinking age to use this book. I am not interested in getting letters or reviews from angry spouses and disappointed readers who were warned right here, right now. If you struggle with day-to-day life, are not meeting basic needs like food, shelter, job, clothing, and healthcare and/or you failed the CAGE test by answering "Yes" to any of the questions and you're still putting alcohol ahead of everything else, my method won't work.

You have to be willing to let go of getting wasted, for good. You have to be solidly anchored in this method. You have to be willing to change your alcohol intake, for good. You will never want to paddle back across the waters of chaos once you land on the new island.

If you are ready to enjoy and not dread drinking, turn the page. Otherwise, I encourage you to get treatment from a behavioral psychologist. I believe Addiction is an Obsessive-Compulsive Self-Destructive Disorder. You'll never see that in a diagnostic manual. I have seen it everywhere throughout my life. It is the subject of every novel I have written. It is my personal and clinical opinion that psychology pathologizes any and all alcohol consumption. They have a zero-tolerance policy for substance use. Yet, they drink their dainty wines and beers with their friends and colleagues. They don't know how to deal with you like I do. I am a reformed drinker. I have made the leap to alcohol enthusiast. If you want to get in the boat and paddle towards the island as I tell you a little bit about my method before you decide, that's fine. Please paddle far enough from your old shore to see the new shore of my island before deciding what to do. Give me a chance to talk you into stopping alcohol from knifing through you. It will. It will chop you down. You can stand there pretending you're not bleeding and falling apart but those of us who can see you will know the truth.

Chapter 1- Your current Island

Your life right now is your current island. Every detail about "you" is the "island" you have landed on. The choices you've made landed you there. Right?

Look around you. Describe your island. Who lives with and around you? Family? Relatives? Friends? Colleagues? How do they feel about you? How do they change around you when you're drunk? When you're angry? How do you act when you're drunk on your island? What do you like about your life? What do you love or cherish? What do you want to get rid of and what would you like to keep? What are your current rules around alcohol? Get out a piece of paper. Go on! Go get it. I will wait. Now, answer all of those questions. Hang on to that data. If you won't answer the questions or bother to write it down, get a refund right now. You're not ready to change. Change requires salt water. It is either sweat from hard work or tears. That's Isak Denisen's philosophy. I agree with him.

Let's assume since you bought this book that alcohol has been problematic.

How do you change it?
Option 1- Quit.
Option 2- Keep drinking the same way, hoping change will occur by chance.
Option 3- Quit for a while then relapse.
Option 4- Quit and substitute addiction or addictive behavior with other drugs or hobbies.
Option 5- Drink more.
Option 6- Regulate alcohol intake. Find limits. Do not exceed limits.

There are many more options but listing them is beyond the scope or intent of this book.

Let's take each option from above and break it down:

*Option 1- Quitting. If you want the best advice about drinking and how to handle it, look no further. You can quit. If it felt good to read that sentence, that is a red flag telling you it has control. Alcohol is a depressant. Alcoholics are self-loathing dysthymics. Alcohol is their manna. If you are at the end of your rope hoping your life is going to improve by chance and you drink like a pirate, you are unreachable. Quit. Stop drinking. Go to rehab or detox before you end up there or in jail. If you don't want rehab, shell out money for a good behavioral therapist to deal with the inevitable depression that will snowball on you once you quit. Plan on staying in treatment of some kind for the rest of your life. Quitting is hard. Good luck. Don't forget to detox if you are a hardcore drinker. Seizures can kill you. Never quit cold turkey. If you don't think death from withdrawal is real, call the hospital and ask them. I would recommend avoiding enabling relationships or ending those you have if you plan on quitting. Be prepared to lose drinking buddies. Be prepared to have cravings and longings. Be prepared to eventually develop an aversion to drinkers. Most of all (if you do quit) stick to it! Do everything you can to avoid relapsing. If you relapse, don't let anybody tell you its no big deal. Bullshit. It is a huge deal. Relapsing drinkers have no business dabbling with my method. You should stay quit. Already been there done that? Tough shit. Go back or go to therapy or both. This is your one and only life. Don't let alcohol destroy it anymore. Stop. The outcomes for addiction are jail, graveyard, rehab, or hospital. It never waivers. It never changes. If you live by the sword, you will die by it. If you walk on white hot coals, you will burn your feet, eventually. Quitting is the best advice I can give you. If you have struggled with alcohol and contemplated getting real help, my method is the wrong choice for you. Quit. Get help. If you fail, go back. Repeat until you regain dignity and integrity.

* Option 2- Keep drinking the same way, hoping change will occur by chance. Guess what? It never will. It never does. It is one of the many illusions in the desert of the alcoholic. It is a shimmering mirage you think you can see from your shore but it does not exist. Go ahead and swim for it. I'll wait. If you bought this book and have read this far, you know in your heart you cannot drink like you have been for the rest of your life. That brings me

conveniently to the main lesson: if you lie to yourself about your drinking problem, you need help. If you admit wholeheartedly that you love drinking but hate being a drunk, you should revisit option one. Most readers will read this book and try to cut back without using the cards. They will fail. If you have gotten to the point where you want to quit but can't say goodbye and want to make a lifelong change in your alcohol intake experience, keep reading. But, know right now, your days of reckless abandon with alcohol are over. Shed your tears and say goodbye. Trust me. You won't miss those days for too long after we fix your drinking experience.

* Option 3- Quit for a while then relapse. This is a major red flag. Relapsing is a huge deal. I am so tired of pop-psychology saying its part of recovery. No, its not. They are colluding with the paying client. Relapsing is a part of recovery like death is a part of dying. If you relapsed you really need to stay away from alcohol and treat your

depression and compulsive behavior. If everybody tells you it will be okay for you to have a few every once in a while, why bother? Just quit for good. There's nothing more annoying than watching a real drunk squirm while craving that third and fourth drink after they zip through the second drink their worn out spouse reluctantly allows them at the Christmas party. They always make fun of themselves and chuckle. To me they are sad and pathetic. If alcohol has gotten to that point for you, stay off of it. Alcoholism does not discriminate. Alcohol doesn't give a damn about how much you made last year. Alcohol doesn't care how good or bad things are going. As long as you keep drinking, Alcohol is happy. Alcohol does not feel sorry for you. I do. Alcohol never says no. Alcohol is always there for you, in times of sorrow and joy. Alcohol is a crutch you rent. It props you up by your liver and makes you a slave animal to it. Fall to your knees or do something that works: cut back. If your drinking problem is causing major life problems, stay off of it. I'm sorry. But, you folks are living proof that lying to yourself about your drinking while everyone else cringes at the truth <u>never</u> <u>works</u>. Relapse is a sign to stay away. Remember when you were a toddler and put your hand on the hot stove? It burned you. Same thing here: relapse is the hot stove. Lying and saying its part of quitting is lying to yourself. If your therapist told you relapse was part of recovery, shame on them. They are colluding with you for your money. You have mastered the art of lying to yourself if you are reading this and are angry at me for exposing you. If you want to see if you are deluded, let someone who knows you read this book with you. Let them answer the questions for you. The truth will prevail. I still love you. I still want you to get help but you need to quit. If you have been to jail, a hospital or a rehab for something addiction related, quit. Why let it cost you more?

* Option 4- Quit and substitute addiction or addictive behavior with other drugs or hobbies. These are the guys who go to AA and drink fifty gallons of coffee while chain smoking. That's less harmful than the guy who quits, pops or snorts

prescription pills, and chain smokes to stave off the alcohol longings. Another guy who quits might get heavy into jogging. That's the way to do it. Substitute constructive hobbies for destructive habits. And, stay off other real drugs. All psychiatric drugs are mind altering. Taking a Valium to calm down during "recovery" is substance abuse. Don't rush out and get a Medical marijuana card once sober from heavy drinking, talk to your regular doctor. Ask questions. Some swear marijuana helps alcoholics stay quit. I don't know but I'd rather you be stoned than drunk driving or fighting while intoxicated. Your history of addiction means you'll probably abuse medical marijuana, be mindful.

* Option 5- Drink More- You might laugh at this option but it happens. Sometimes, you reach a point where your drinking makes you stop and reflect. If you are reading this sentence, you are there now. This book might trigger you to say, screw it. It might make you think you don't need anybody telling you what to do, etc. You can

handle your drinking. You don't need this bullshit book to cut back. You can do it. You don't care if so-and-so doesn't like the way you act when you're drinking. Well, that's okay. You are just resisting. The proof will remain in the behavioral pudding. If you continue to drink the way you have been, you will remain unreachable. Everybody that you rage at is right about you. You have an attitude problem because you are terrified of living without being able to party any time you please as hard as you'd like. I understand. But, you have got to do something. Don't go out after throwing this book or getting a refund and get hammered. Just don't. Start the method instead. Great news Bruisers, it starts now!

* Option 6- Regulate alcohol intake. Find limits. Do not exceed limits.

"The Card Carrying Method of Harm Reduction for Drinkers"

Welcome to my island! You made it! (Insert pat on the back). I'm proud of you for braving the waters. Don't worry. Being on the island is voluntary. You can leave anytime you want. No one will stop you. No one will beg you to reconsider. You can always come back as long as you didn't break one of our rules.

Rules for the Island:
1. You cannot drink and drive ever again. If you are drinking and driving at all with any vehicle, stop. Say goodbye to drunk driving. It is a lethal gamble we no longer take. If you ever drink and drive, you are banished from the island.
2. Never are you to drink more than four days in a row, for the first six months. From Monday to Sunday you get four drinking credits. Use them or lose them. No rollovers. This is not a cellphone with rollover

minutes, this is an island rule. Anyone who breaks the four credits rule will be banished. No exceptions.

3. You can only drink wine and beer. No liquor. No shots of liquor. No mixed drinks. No food with hard alcohol in it. No mouthwash or tinctures with alcohol in it. If you drink or consume liquor and are expecting my method to help you, it won't. This is a beer and wine only island. Say goodbye to liquor or swim back to your island. Don't try to slip high alcohol content beers under the radar, you're lying to yourself again. Same thing with big, full wine glasses. Drink a pint of beer or a ten ounce glass of wine. Anything more is cheating the system but more importantly, cheating yourself. No liquor allowed in any quantity or form. No exceptions. Liquor unleashes madness too often, sorry.

4. You will create cards to track your drinking from now on. You will need twenty business cards to make your cards. Take twelve business cards and number them big, 1-12 with a sharpee. These are your beer cards. For each of the twelve cards you

numbered write the word "BEER" across the bottom. On the sixth card write the word "USUAL AMOUNT" on it. Why? Because your goal is to normalize your drinking, a usual amount of beer is a six-pack. We are using that standard as a marker. On the 9th beer card, write the word "Maximum." This is another marker or milestone. You have drank one and a half six-packs. On the twelfth card write the word "LAST." Your Beer cards are now complete. You have twelve business cards numbered from 1-12. On the sixth card it says "Usual" on the ninth card it says "Maximum" and on the twelfth card it says "Last." When you drink beer from now on, you will try to stop at six. If you are behaving yourself, you can have nine. But, no matter what, you stop at twelve, for the first six months. Now, take the other eight cards and number them, 1-8. Write the word "WINE" on each card's bottom. On the fourth card, write the word "USUAL AMOUNT" on the eighth card write the word "LAST." With wine, we point out the fourth glass since that is the equivalent of one bottle of wine. A standard we will use to move towards.

So, now you are holding twenty business cards. Twelve of them are for beer and eight of them are for wine. Find a small see-through plastic ziplock to keep them in. Or, put a rubber band around your cards.

5.   Rules for using the cards to track your drinking: for the first six months, you are to only drink a maximum of twelve beers or eight glasses of wine. Each time you get another beer or glass of wine, you flip to the next numbered card to track your intake. Every time you go drinking, carry your cards with you. You are responsible for keeping up with how many you've had from now on. You can mix and match wine and beer but each wine card counts for two beer cards. In simpler terms, you can never exceed, in any combination, twelve beers or eight glasses of wine, total. Anyone who exceeds the generous limit will be banished from the island. To drill this point in all the way: for the first six months, the absolute most you are allowed to drink is twelve beers or eight glasses of wine. Two six packs or two bottles of wine. Mix and

match but don't go over the limit.
Remember: if you are mixing wine and
beer, wine cards count as two beers.
Get it? Got it? Good. Now, never ever
break that rule. No one needs to drink
more than two sixers or two bottles of
wine. The reason my method works is
because it is based in drinking reality. If
you drink that thirteenth beer or open
that third bottle of wine, you are rolling
the dice too many times. I think chances
are you are going to suffer. Stop drinking
like there's no tomorrow and you will see
a shift in your life. You can leave your
anxiety. You are finally in control. You
will find your limits and reduce your
drinking by starting with a maximum and
tapering down. That is the secret. Yes,
you will still get really drunk. Your goal is
to throw away cards until you find your
limit. You are simplifying your drinking
experience. You are stopping liquor
altogether. You are allowing yourself a
maximum of either two six packs or two
bottles of wine. And, you are only
drinking four days a week, for the first
six months. Try it. I guarantee you
success, if you are willing to stick to it
and taper down until you find your magic
number by six months time. What do I

mean by magic number? Your magic number is the cut-off card. It serves as the marker for when you are at the peak of your desired buzz. In the beginning, you will use the cards and drink through all of them. Eventually, you will have a bad night and deduct a card from your stack. Do that until you find your number and stick to it. Don't worry, you are supposed to screw up and have bad times until you find your magic number. No one is perfect. You are setting the realistic goal to never exceed a twelve pack of beer or two bottles of wine. You will invariably get drunk and even with the cards in place, you will act like a drunk idiot. Every time you do, you lose a card, for good. No exceptions. If you don't taper down, you are abusing the system. You aren't hurting me, you're hurting yourself. Stop doing that. The other major important thing is not to forget to flip your cards when you start a new drink! I recommend keeping your cards on you anytime you go out or drink at home. Make a couple of sets. Why do we use business cards? Because you can be discreet with them. No one will notice or care what you keep doing every time you get another beer.

Trust me. If you are self-conscious about it, go flip them in the bathroom. If a friend busts you flipping cards, tell them you are tracking calories. Or, tell them the truth! Say, "I'm tired of alcohol ruining my life. I've decided to cut myself off and this is how I know when to stop drinking." You are on a new island. If you stay here and let the cards method have a real chance, it will change you. You will wonder why you stayed on your island for so long when this one was here all along. You will lament your bad drunk times. You will cringe thinking about all the times you went to the bar and drank as many as you could before last call. You will learn that the cards force you to face how much you're drinking. That's why this method works. It eats away at your conscience when you screw up. You feel your anxiety. It reinforces you to halt excessive drinking to avoid the unpleasent feeling of chaos. Another reward is financial. You will save so much money on going out to drink. You can go out more often once you learn to stop. You will not believe how different this new island feels. All you have to do is not drink more than four days a week and never drink more than two sixers or two bottles of wine then taper down by six months. The rest will fall into place. My island will become your island. Once you discover your cut-off card, tears of joy will drown the old shore you dwelled on all those shameful years before.

Chapter 3- Fine tuning (Read this chapter after eight weeks of using the cards)

Now that you have been on the island, for a while, you've probably noticed something. Twelve beers is a LOT of alcohol. Two bottles of wine is a LOT of wine for one person. This is where tapering comes in. The goal is to drink for a while and fine tune your cards. Maybe ten beers is enough now that you've cut back? Maybe six glasses of wine is the perfect amount for you? Whatever it is, find it. Find your magic number. Take unneeded cards and tear them up. Customize your stack. You will love being an alcohol enthusiast instead of a problematic, compulsive, gluttonous alcoholic. You will finally have fun and more money when you go out. People have horrible drunk nights due to getting way too intoxicated! How do you stop it? Regulate and track how much you drink. The other critical step is to STOP drinking shots and liquor.

The pitfall of my method, (besides expecting you to stick with the method for good) is that alcoholics lie to

themselves and rationalize drinking.
What do I mean?
Real drunks will read this book, make
the cards, then find ways to rationalize
drinking more than they are allotted.
They will fail and eventually chunk the
cards. They will hang their head, at first,
but will soon return to problem drinking.
They will feel worse about their drinking
because they failed at regulating it.
Other drunks will violate the rule about
only drinking four days a week for the
first six months. They will find a way to
excuse themselves from that critical
rule. They will fail at my method. If you
lie to yourself and violate these rules,
don't come crying to me. I warned you
about cheating yourself. Alcohol will trick
you and tease you into submission.
That's how it hooked you in the first
place. Recognize that and stop it. Or,
quit drinking. The secret to my method is
you. If you don't follow it, you failed, not
the method. If I gave you a parachute
and pushed you off a cliff, you would not
die if you used the parachute. No one
can refute the validity of a method
aimed at reducing alcohol intake if the
user consistently demonstrates a
change in their drinking behavior and

adheres to the use of the cards to cut back and monitor alcohol intake. My method is fail-proof. It will work, provided the user adheres to it.

The bottom-line with my method is that you have to commit to YOURSELF. Forget about everybody else. If you are cutting back drinking to appease a spouse or loved one, you will fail. If someone gave you this book, take the hint. They are worn out from dealing with you. If you simply cannot keep up with the cards and the only drinking four days a week rule for the first six months, then strongly consider quitting. My island permits up to a twelve pack of beer or two bottles of wine. Do you really need more than that to get buzzed? If so, my method will not work for you. I was a therapist for ten years. Trust me. The worst lies people tell are the one's they tell themselves. You ain't fooling me! I have sat across from you, shaking my head in disbelief, as you ramble on about how you're okay with your drinking and you're getting better, etc. Its bullshit. I know it. You know it. And, if you don't or can't stop lying to yourself, I can't help you. You need to quit or do rehab. What do you want people to say at your funeral? That you were a hopeless drunk loser or that you got your life together and cut back? You decide.

Why drink at all, if its gotta be so regimented?

Let's face it. Drinking can be fun. We love the good times. But, it can also be deadly. Impaired judgement, arguments, fighting, crying, and being stubborn while intoxicated are all recipes for disaster. Suicide, disease, depression, fatal drunk driving, murder, robbery, and injury are all likely outcomes when you have no restraint with alcohol. I am offering you restraint. Use it. If I tossed you over the edge of a ship during a storm but tossed you a lifeline, would you take it or let the storm drown you? Stop flailing in the storm, here's the lifesaver. Grab it. Take control of alcohol and become an enthusiast, not an insatiable addict who rattles their chains at the closing of the bar. You will be set free from the slave driver you imbibe.

Other notes:

* <u>Never</u> <u>drink</u> <u>without</u> <u>your</u> <u>cards</u>. Never allow yourself a night of no cards. Never think you can quit counting drinks just because you got good at it and made progress. Never stop using the cards to help youat home and while out. People with asthma need an inhaler. You are an alcohol enthusiast, you need your cards. Get it?

* Be careful about flipping cards when going out to bars and clubs. You should be prepared to keep up with your cards, no matter what. Don't forget to flip to the next card each and every time you get a drink. Don't forget! You will! Trust me!

* Get your friends to cut back with you or ask you what number you are on when you act like an idiot. Note: if you are still acting like a drunk idiot, even after switching to the cards, you need to quit, not taper off. You aren't doing it right. You can get buzzed but no more getting completely wasted. If you are drinking all twelve beers and doing that four instead of seven days a week, nice start. You have some control instead of

none but let's get down to a reasonable number of drinks for you. No more crazy nights. Remember the whole point of this island is to leave your old island, forever. If you are acting <u>exactly</u> <u>the</u> <u>same</u>, despite cutting back, and tapering off on your drinks, you need to quit.

* If you switch to this method and are still <u>upsetting</u> <u>those</u> <u>around</u> <u>you</u> after tapering down, you need to quit. If you create tension everytime you crack open a beer, you need to quit. Pay attention to that dread filling up the room. You have probably caused everyone to walk on eggshells for too long around you when you're drunk. They are worn out. Even though you've cut back, your efforts may be too little, too late. Listen to your critics. They will tell you the truth. Alcohol is not for everybody. You might be one of those people. This guideline is for the people who act like jerks when they drink. Cutting back doesn't impact your being a jerk. Stop being a jerk and quit. We are tired of dealing with you. You don't enjoy drinking, you ruin it for everybody. Say goodbye to your bad attitude <u>and</u> alcohol. You lost the privilege to drink by acting like an

asshole for too many years. Cutting back doesn't erase the past. Beg for forgiveness, be nice, and stay clean. Maybe you will become tolerable? That's all you can hope for after the Hell you've put us through. Nobody likes a drunk asshole, especially one who has cut back but retains the poor attitude. You can't have both. Lose the attitude. Lose the booze. Ask for forgiveness and be nicer, for good. Stay in anger management and therapy for the rest of your life. Don't congratulate me on helping you cut back, if you are still an asshole, drunk or sober. I can't stand you like everybody else. I'm not your ally. I'm your enemy. You are cutting back to appease those around you but you really need to stop being a jerk. Get help. Drunk assholes are master manipulators of unsuspecting enabling-types. Don't get duped by one. If you are a parent who drinks and your kids hate you, I'm talking to you. Take the Asshole test if you are unsure where you stand. Have someone who will be honest with you read this section and tell you if that's your problem. The truth will prevail. But, if you're an asshole, the truth about you probably won't matter now since it never has. Some things can't be fixed. Don't let your poor attitude, past or present, keep you from change. What doesn't bend breaks. Stop letting anger keep the real you from those you love. Let go. How do you want to be remembered after you're dead? As someone who never got it that they were an unbearable asshole or someone who changed? All we want is for you to be nice. Do it.

* If you really have tried this method and it works, be ready for depression to surface. Actually, you should let that depression be a sign of progress. Maybe you should feel bad! Think about all the things you have lost and ruined due to irresponsible drinking. Shouldn't you pay attention and change your life? No one else is going to do it for you. Once you switch to regulated drinking, you will look back on how you used to be and get depressed. Count on it. If it gets to be too much, quit. But, expect it to consume you. You are mourning your past. Let it go and party with limits, from now on. Let it be a trial and tribulation not a testament. Break the pain cycle. Take control of alcohol or quit. This book

started out saying one thing: giving up is something you do for somebody else, letting go is something you do for yourself. Why are you cutting back? For you? Or, to get them to shut up and leave you alone about your drinking? If you are in it for them, you will fail. Be in it for you or quit.

My method is a last resort. It is an island. You can stay here the rest of your life, if you follow the rules. We party hard but we make it home safe and sane. Join the party but know that this island is not for everybody. If you go back to your old shores, you will see what I mean. Never leave this place and it will shower you with life. Lie to yourself or break a rule and you are banished. If you can't take the rigors of the method, then you need to quit. And, most of all, anybody reading this should be in behavioral therapy.

I am giving you a skeleton by eliminating your problem drinking, it is up to you and a cognitive-behavioral therapist to flesh out the rest. Be prepared for them to dismiss my book and method if you should have quit but cut back instead or

if you go to a psychodynamic/
psychoanalytic therapist.

Follow-up questions and answers:

Question: I am a problem drinker, I guess. I have a habit of buying a couple of six packs during football day games to drink with friends. We usually go to the bar for the rest of the night, after the games. I get as wasted as I can until they make us leave. I used to stop drinking at three in the morning but I violate that rule all the time. I don't care. If we can, we go to the store and buy more beer after the bar closes. I probably end up drinking at least 18-22 beers. Should I start counting my drinks before trying the cards?

Answer: No. Do not bother counting. My first response is to tell you to quit drinking. You should go to the doctor and get checked out. Heavy drinking like that does damage. Sign up for therapy, too.

Question: My girlfriends and I love tequila. We have a longstanding tradition of drinking margarita pitchers every Thursday at my local bar. I can't say no. I only let myself drink four. But, I got written up at work for being late again on a Friday morning. What should I do? I like some beer but hate wine.

Answer: Sadly, you must say goodbye to your beloved pitchers. Find a beer you like and announce to the group your new plan. Heck, show them the cards! Whatever you do, stop drinking liquor. Liquor is dangerous and impossible to predict and count. It is cleaner on your system but my plan works for beer and wine only. Why? Liquor manifests too unpredictably in people. I recommend quitting it, for good. Slow sip a good Scotch if you must but leave this book to the wine and beer crowd. Liquor scares me in large quantities in any body. Large or small. Male or female. Liquor unleashes the untamable beast from the depths of Hell. No thanks! Switch to beer and/or wine for good and get on the cards.

Question: I have a wild group of buddies here at school. We love videogames. We love to drink while playing for hours at a time. We take turns going to the corner store until it closes. I probably pound around 15-20 beers on a Saturday night. We drink like that five nights a week, sometimes six. I do shots first thing in the morning to get the party started on hang-over days. Sometimes when we run out of booze, I sneak a couple of swigs from the Listerine bottle. But, we are twenty-two! We are young, so its okay.

Answer: Young friend, trust me. You need to quit. Why wait for something bad to happen? You are pounding that many beers that many days a week, using an eye-opener to start the day, and drinking mouthwash to stave off the shakes. You are an alcoholic. Stop and get help.

Question- I love wine. I work at a wine bar and must do tastings. How do I calculate how many I have had? Outside of work, I drink between three and four bottles of wine at least two nights a week.

Answer: You need to estimate what a glass is while erring on the side of caution. I would say three or four samples equals a glass. Use unimpaired judgement to decide your rule. Wine tastings are the least desirable place to be a card carrier. Its too hard. If you must, err on the side of caution. As far as your drinking three to four bottles, I would say you should definitely limit yourself to two and taper down. Three to four bottles of wine is 12-16 glasses of wine. That's way too much for even two nights a week.

Question: I live on a bustling street with three awesome bars. My friends and I love to meet up and start at one bar and drink our way down the line. I think most nights I end up having four to six beers and a couple of shots of yagermeister. I don't have any problems in my life. I have a loving girlfriend, a steady high paying job, and never get out of control. My life is happy and my friends are all cool and fun. Should I use the cards?

Answer: No. If you are having fun and are functioning fine, why rock the boat? A paid Psyhotherapist might say alcohol is a problem for you. I disagree. I look at global functioning for cases like yours. I wouldn't waste time on specific behaviors that are within normal limits and are not creating problems.

Question: I have a group of friends that are pushy. We slam shots all night long on weekends. Pitchers of beer never stop coming. My wife took my daughter and left. I lost my job and feel suicidal. The boys tell me they will take care of me and get me through this. We are investment bankers and make good money. I would never dream of drinking during the work week. I guess I'm a weekend warrior who goes to battle at the bar. I took a girl home last week and had unprotected sex. I haven't done that in years and now I'm willing to cut back on my drinking. How do I handle peer pressure with my friends to keep pounding drinks?

Answer: I think you should find a seasoned behavioral therapist and get help. Suicidal thoughts are symptoms of lethal stress. You are drinking heavily, have lost a high paying job, have lost contact and time with your kid and should quit, not cutback. I think drinking has become central to your life. I would strongly suggest stopping. If you want your family back, you have to say goodbye to drinking.

Question: I am twenty-four. I am engaged to a baseball addict. We go to all the home games and drink beer all nine innings. I can't take it after a few big ones but my future hubby cheers me on. Last Thursday, I ended up throwing up in the car on the way home. I'm embarrassed and disgusted by my mistake. But, I don't want to quit. Nothing like this has ever happened to me before. I have no other major issues or complaints about my life.

Answer: Finding support from a self-professed addict like your guy might get dicey. Are you sure this guy you are deeply in love with is good for you? For instance, how much does he drink per game? Per week? Remember what I said about drinking and relationships: stay away from enablers. Otherwise, you should try the cards but be forewarned: you need to taper down. Puking is a sign of over-the-top drunkenness. Don't ever let it get that way again. Stop at the buzz and see what number you are on before carefully decide what to do. Don't stay with your fiancé if he won't support you in cutting back.

Question: I am twenty-seven and a full-time rocker. I play drums in four different bands. I use beer as fuel for networking, making business contacts, and to stay confident around all the girls. I probably drink more nights than not. I have been known to "check out" sometimes when I'm really hammered. I get quiet and pass out. My bandmates tease me for zoning out after shows on the couch in the studio but I wear myself out driving all over the place. Drinking is a huge part of my job and lifestyle. Sometimes I don't want to drink but I kinda have to if certain chicks show up or some of the local club owners are buying. I live alone in a studio apartment with my cat. I make enough to get by on. Most of my money is paying the cost to live my party-hard lifestyle! I've got to do something. I passed out in my car and ran off the road last week. Thankfully, I forgot to zip my cymbal bag. My hi-hats slid out and made a crash that woke me up. No one was around. I got myself back on the road. I sped home wide awake. It scared me. I have rent coming up and four gigs next week. What should I do?

Answer: The most urgent thing to stop is your drinking and driving. You have to completely stop doing that. You will eventually kill one of us or yourself. So, first things first, stop drunk driving. If you refuse to quit and get help, you must at least agree to leave all vehicles alone. My guess is that won't work for you. You have to use the car to get to paid gigs. So, I suggest you get treatment from a therapist to address how to handle social pressure around drinking. You really should quit. Passing out is a major red flag. It is your body shutting down from too much. You will eventually hit your head or get some other injury or you will end up in the hospital with some alcohol related disease from drinking too much.

Question: I have been using the card method. It is amazing. I used to go out with my coworkers after work most days of the week. We would bar hop and stay out late. Nobody ever got too wasted. We always made it to work on time the next day. My problem was financial. I knew I was in trouble when I had to use my credit card at the bar because my checking account was overdrawn while I waited for my direct deposit from work to show up at midnight. I felt like such a lush. That was when I decided to use the cards. I followed your method and stopped drinking and driving. I began taking the bus on the four days I decided to go out. I stopped drinking the occasional vodka cranberry. I started with twelve beer cards and am now down to just five. I can't believe after all these years it only takes five beers over the course of a night for me to have a great buzz, a great time, and still retain my senses. I've saved a ton of money by drinking less and only going out three nights a week instead of four or five. Occasionally, on Friday nights, I like to allow myself to drink eight or nine beers. I only do it at my favorite bar and it is my reward for cutting back, is that okay?

Answer:

The rules of the island are not violated by your built in reward system. As long as you are still functioning, are okay with your Friday night treat, and are still firmly in control then enjoy yourself.

There is a small chance that having that ninth beer will sometimes push you too far. If it does, tear that card up and throw it away. If you are happy, cutting back or have cut back, and are following the rules, feel free to build in little rewards. After all, we still want to have fun drinking with friends. The whole point of this method is to maximize fun and minimize harm. If you are okay with the changes you have made and are sticking to them, have fun with it!

Dedication-- To Dr. Drew Pinsky: I am convinced. You were sent from the heavens to heal those afflicted with deadly addiction. You are not from this dark, cruel world ruled by Apathy. You are an Angel. You are a savior in white light. You are my hero, bro. This book is for you. I know most drinkers should quit but what about those who can cut back and function? Just saying... My contribution to your cause will be one of harm reduction. Not everybody needs to quit, some just need to get better at controlling themselves. This book will help identify who can handle the necessary discipline versus those who need treatment. You take the lambs, I'll take the sheep. I love you, man. You rule. Keep doing what you do. All of us young psychologists are watching. You are a beacon for those in pain from addiction. I see your light from all the way up here in San Francisco. I'm surfing one for you, brother. Peace. -- Love, Jake Ray.

And, to all the victims of drunk drivers who've died...this book is for you. I'm sorry it took me this long to edit and re-release this book. I want your lives to be remembered and for the world to change. Eradicating problem drinking and getting people to stay off the road after any alcohol is my goal with this book. It will never bring you back but hopefully my method can make drinkers think twice before driving because they aren't as intoxicated due to cutting back? If it saves one life, it will have been worth publishing. I'm sorry selfish people let their addictions take you away from us. Your death was not in vain. I'm giving people a new tool to help prevent and reduce drunk driving. Maybe someone who reads it will quit, cut back, or at least not get behind the wheel next time they drink?

NOTES FROM MONTH 1:

_____

NOTES FROM MONTH 2: